Consumed Life

A Woman's Guide to Studying God's Word Every Day

Michelle Rabon

ISBN 978-0-692-19302-0

2018 Displaying Grace. All rights reserved. All contents of this study are copyrighted and cannot be copied or reproduced for any purposes without prior written permission.

Printed in the U.S.A.

Scripture quotations are from The Holy Bible, English Standard Version (ESV), Copyright © 2001 by Crossway, a publishing ministry of Good News Publishers. Used by permission. All rights reserved.

Scripture quotations marked CSB have been taken from the Christian Standard Bible®, Copyright © 2017 by Holman Bible Publishers. Used by permission. Christian Standard Bible® and CSB® are federally registered trademarks of Holman Bible Publishers.

Scripture quotations marked "NIV" are taken from The Holy Bible, New International Version®, (NIV®) Copyright © 1973, 1978, 1984, 2011 by Biblica, Inc.® Used by permission. All rights reserved worldwide.

Table of Contents

Learning to Live by the Word .... pg. 4
How to Use this Study Guide .... pg. 6
Consumed Life Commitment .... pg. 7
Personal Inventory .... pg. 9

Part One - The Study Basics
Four Steps to Bible Study .... pg. 13
Preparing Our Hearts for His Word .... pg. 14
The Five W's of Bible Study .... pg. 17
Quality, Not Quantity .... pg. 19
Bible Translation Chart .... pg. 21
Come All Who Are Weary .... pg. 23
Books of the Bible .... pg. 25

Part Two - How to Study Your Bible
More than Words .... pg. 29
Verse Mapping .... pg. 31
SOAP Method .... pg. 32
Color Coding .... pg. 33
Bible Color Chart .... pg. 35
Word Study .... pg. 37
Character Study .... pg. 38
Character Study Worksheet .... pg. 39
Inductive Study Method .... pg. 41
Topical Study Method .... pg. 43
Homiletics Study Method .... pg. 44

Part Three - Live it out
Practical Quiet Time .... pg. 48
Bridging the Gap .... pg. 50
Defense Against Distractions .... pg. 52
Recommended Resources .... pg. 56
Fresh Start Reading Plan .... pg. 57

Learning to live by the Word...

When I was a child my interaction with God's Word was limited to occasional Sunday School classes, sporadic Vacation Bible schools in the summer, and stories my grandparents shared with me. During my teenage years, my mom signed herself and I, up for a discipleship class at our local church, and with it she gifted me with what I call my first "real" Bible. That class became my first attempt at studying the Bible for myself.

For the first time, I opened God's Word seeking to know more. Unfortunately, I failed to find what I was looking for as a teen in a class full of adults, and I never continued. Other aspects of my teenage life became more important and that Bible sat on my shelf for years before it would ever be opened again.

Press fast forward and you find a young woman, a fresh college drop out with her life in disarray, living on her own with very little desperately hoping to make it through what felt like rock bottom. Little did I know the neighbors in the apartment next to mine would share Truth with me, a truth I had heard before, but for the first time understood. The truth that Jesus loved me so much that He went to a cross for the purpose of redeeming my life, my soul and eternal standing. A dark veil that covered my heart lifted with this knowledge and in the days that followed I fully surrendered my life to Christ, and accepted the greatest gift I have ever received.

Forgiveness.

In the days that followed I searched for my "real" Bible, the one long packed away, lost somewhere in the past. The only one that I could manage to find was a Children's Bible. I didn't care, I just needed the Word. Even in my infancy as a Christian I felt the pull of God's Word on my life. It was far different from those teen years, my bones ached to hear from God almost instantly after I became a Christian.

I was like a newborn who had an instant need to be nourished, so I wore down the binding of that Children's Bible for weeks.

Eventually I found my "real" Bible and as I type these words, it rests in my lap, a little tattered and worn. It has been highlighted with care and covered with tears. The margins hold notes and truths that God revealed to me during those early years of faith. When I hold it in my hands there is a stirring in me; it reminds me of a rescue so great that it altered the course of my life forever.
As a teenager it was just a book, but in my early twenties it was the life support that allowed me to survive.

I will never turn back to those days without hope because of the Holy, Living, Breathing Word of God. I have seen the power of what opening your Bible can do. Not just in my own life but in the lives of women I have taught for many years. I have watched their eyes open to the incredible power of His Word and seen Him awaken the Spirit within them. I have witnessed women come to faith, and see their callings rise; all because of God's powerful Word.

God's Word testifies of its own power as it is revealed to us through the Old and New Testaments. It is breathed out to us with power and purpose, *"All Scripture is inspired by God and is profitable for teaching, for rebuking, for correcting, for training in righteousness, so that the man of God may be complete, equipped for every good work."* (2 Timothy 3:16-17, CSB)

The Holy Scriptures are alive! *"For the word of God is living and effective and sharper than any double-edged sword, penetrating as far as the separation of soul and spirit, joints and marrow. It is able to judge the thoughts and intentions of the heart."* (Hebrews 4:12, CSB)

His Word will not return empty handed because it is sent out with the purpose of growth and change. It will do exactly what God has purposed for it to do. *"For just as rain and snow fall from heaven and do not return there without saturating the earth and making it germinate and sprout, and providing seed to sow and food to eat, so my word that comes from my mouth will not return to me empty, but it will accomplish what I please and will prosper in what I send it to do."* (Isaiah 55:10-11, CSB)

When we know its purpose, we will understand its power.

As His daughter, you crave His Word, you desire to know more of God. And, you know Him by opening the pages of Scripture and allowing God to speak to you.

Consumed Life isn't just a book or Bible study; it is a resource help you navigate studying your Bible every day. Each page is filled with practical tips and study essentials. Whether you are a new believer or seasoned saint, I pray you will discover your love for God's Word as you open its pages.

My prayer over you is this, that God would give you a heart to learn, a mind to understand, and a spirit to help you live out the words you read.

Grab your Bible and let's jump in…together.

Michelle

How to use this study guide:

Consumed Life isn't your average Bible Study Guide. It will be your Bible study best friend and go-to resource for years to come.

To use this guide effectively, you will need to write in it, mark it, fold corners, rip out pages, cover it with sticky notes and bend its spine. This book was not created to remain a work of art, but a well loved tool in your arsenal.

Pour over each page, tip, tool and encouragement.
Put into practice what you learn and come back again and again.
Try each method of study and examine what each one means to you, and how you can use it in your daily Bible study time.

This book is broken into three parts:

Study Basics -
The study basics are only scratch the surface of studying Scripture. If you learn nothing else from this book, let the study basics wash over you and change how you see the Bible. We cannot treat the Word as a genie in our magic lamp; our Bibles should always be studied with purpose.

How to Study the Bible -
There are so many different ways to study your Bible. What method will you use? This section gives you an overview of the different methods available to you and how to use them. (It is by no means a comprehensive list of study methods.)

Study Application -
How do I apply what I read? In this section we will talk about application and how to allow Scripture to saturate our lives in practical ways.

At the end of the book you will find a Fresh Start Bible Reading Plan to help you jump in with both feet. This thirty-day plan is a great way to get started in the Word every day.

Want even more teaching? Find our online companion course at
www.displaying-grace1.teachable.com

Consumed Life Commitment

Now that we are in this together, let's make a commitment.

Each page of this book was created with purpose to help you. Practical tips and teaching assist you in getting the most out of your time in Scripture each day. We will wrestle through the personal, as well as the academic. More than that however, we will seek God with our whole heart. We are all in.

I commit to finishing this Bible study, making time each day to open my Bible, pray, and journal.

I commit to believing the best of myself and my ability, because God sees the best in me.

I will trust God to provide the wisdom and understanding I need.

I will trust the Spirit that dwells within me to lead me to Truth.

I will not get hung up on trivial things, but will ask God to provide clarity to my convictions.

I will share with at least one person each week about what God is teaching me in Scripture, and how His Word is changing me.

Signature & Date : _____

Personal Inventory

What keeps you from being in God's Word on a daily basis?

_____
_____
_____

Do you believe not being in the Word daily affects how you live day to day?

_____
_____
_____

When you sit down to study the Word, what are your greatest distractions?

_____
_____
_____

How do you think you can remedy the distractions around you? (Example; change the time of day or location, remove your to do list, etc.)

_____
_____
_____

What do you hope to gain from completing this Bible study guide?

_____
_____
_____

Notes

Part One: The Study Basics

Four Steps to Bible Study

There are four basic steps to Bible study. No matter what method you use in your daily quiet time. These same four steps will be consistent each time.

Pray

We cannot open God's Word without first opening our minds and hearts to what He has to say to us. Just like appliances cannot work without being plugged into a power source, we cannot hope to gain knowledge of the Word without being plugged into our Power Source. As you begin your study time ask God to teach you by His Holy Spirit and open your eyes to the teachings of His Word, looking for His story rather than your own in its pages.

Read

Read, reread, and read again. When we sit down to God's Word whether we are studying a passage or full chapter, we need to allow God's Word time to sink deep in our hearts. When studying Scripture use multiple translations of the Bible to help you understand what you are reading.

Write

As you read, make notes. The Bible study method you use will determine the style of notes you make as you study. A good general rule is to write down repeated phrases and words. Also note commands, warnings, and who is speaking. See Part Two: How to Study Your Bible on page 27 for more about different Bible study methods.

Apply

Application is a process, one that starts in our heart and radiates out to our behavior. Scripture isn't about us, it is about God. The purpose of Scripture is to teach us about God. Learning about Him changes our character, which equips us to fulfill our purpose and calling.

"So faith comes from hearing, and hearing through the word of Christ." (Romans 10:17, ESV)

Preparing our Hearts for His Word

When we sit down to study God's Word, we should always begin with prayer. Prayer is the anchor in which our hearts and minds connect to the Spirit of God. We cannot expect to learn from the very Words of God unless we have sought Him first.

There is heart preparation that must be done if we are to gain a deeper understanding of His Truth. No matter how much effort we put into it on our own, we must first allow God to teach us as we must seek after His wisdom. (James 1:5)

Here is a prayer example you can follow or create your own in the blank space.

Lord,
I humble myself before you knowing that I am unable in my flesh to understand the fullness of your Truth. Father, ignite the Spirit within me to teach me your Holy Word. Teach me Lord that I may live out your commands. In Jesus name, Amen

(Scripture used - Psalm 119)

Your Prayer

_____
_____
_____
_____
_____
_____

Bible Study tip #1

Tackling one book of the Bible at a time, one chapter at a time, is a great way to grasp the whole of Scripture. It also protects us from taking verses and passages out of context.

The Five W's of Bible Study

Who -

Who wrote it?
Who was it written to?
Who are the major characters?
Who are the people mentioned in the passage?

What -

What are the main events taking place?
What are the major teachings?
What is the behavior of the people?

When -

When was it written?
When did the events take place? (Past)
When will the events take place? (Future)

Where -

Where did it happen?
Where was it written?
Where will it happen?

Why -

Why was it written?
Why is it important to the overarching story of the Gospel?

Notes

Quality, Not Quantity

I overslept again.
My youngest is down with the stomach bug.
Health issues.
Busy with work.

The list could go on and on of the things that interrupt our life and keep us from our time in the Word. There are things that happen beyond our control that deter and derail us. "I don't have time," is one of the statements I hear most often as I teach women to open their Bibles. In fact, it was my own reason for far too long.

There was something about the combination of factors in my life that kept me from opening my Bible. I know now more than anything the enemy sought to blind me concerning my time in order to keep me from unleashing the power that I held within my hands.

Some seasons we create our own reasons for not opening the Word, and other seasons we are truly hindered from our quiet time. But, no matter where we find ourselves we will ALWAYS have time to tuck truth into our hearts.

Personally, I have learned to make it accessible by keeping a pocket Bible in my purse or accessing a Bible app on my phone and having it read to me. I also adjust my sleeping habits to make room for quiet time. Ask God to show you where you waste time, or where you have been blinded to moments that could be spent with Him.

You see, at the end of the day it is about quality, not quantity.

Our amount of time in the Word each day doesn't determine our level of faith. It is, however, what God teaches us when we reach for His breathed out Words that matters the most. We can read those Words all day and never be changed until we let them get under our skin and into our soul. The choice is yours.

Quality will change us, if we open our Bibles and let it speak.

When we bind ourselves with legalistic rules such as; requiring ourselves to study so many minutes a day, at a certain time only, or only one version, etc., we will find being in the Word a chore rather than a treasure. Every time we open it we receive a gift, the gift of Truth.

The purpose of studying Scripture is to know who God is and His Gospel. As we walk through life more equipped knowing His purpose for our lives; we can walk confidently in all things.

When we know who God is we are better moms, wives, sisters, and friends.

Do you remember that "real" Bible I told you about? The one that my mother gave me? It is worn and tear stained but within its pages I learned who God is and, in turn, what my purpose is. It was over that very Bible God called me to ministry, serving women with every bit of my heart.

There is another Bible that sits on my desk. One I never open for fear it will fall apart. The tape that holds the binding together is brittle and every corner is torn; the pages are wrinkled from the precious hands that held it for twenty-three years.

My grandmother's Bible tells a story. Tucked inside of Deuteronomy 31 is the newspaper clipping noting the death of her husband. She placed it there near a highlighted reminder, "The Lord Himself goes before you and will be with you; he will never leave you nor forsake you. Do not be afraid; do not be discouraged" (Deuteronomy 31:8, NIV). Above the verse she wrote, "Do not fear."

So many verses are colored in red colored pencil, underlined, and small notes are tucked throughout. Her Bible was her life source and the same book I opened and read to her during her final months of life. My grandmother knew where the Truth was found and the value of quality, not quantity of time in His precious book.

Quality reveals worn, marked pages. Let us seek to be women of quality over quantity.

Bible Translation Comparison Chart

{Interlinear or Word for Word}

↑

- NASB
- AMP
- ESV
- RSV
- KJV
- NKJV
- CSB
- NRSV
- NAB
- NJB
- NIV
- NLT
- NIrV
- CEV
- LIVING
- THE MESSAGE

↓

{Paraphrase or Thought for Thought}

What does interlinear mean?

_____
_____
_____

What does paraphrase mean?

_____
_____
_____

What versions do you prefer?

_____
_____
_____

Why are those your versions of choice?

_____
_____
_____

Are there any versions you would like to look into?

_____
_____
_____

Why do you believe it is important to understand the difference of the translations?

_____
_____
_____

Come, all who are weary...

"Are you tired?
Worn out?
Burned out on religion?
Come to me.
Get away with me and you'll recover your life.
I'll show you how to take a real rest.
Walk with me and work with me -
Watch how I do it.
Learn the unforced rhythms of grace.
I wont lay anything heavy or ill-fitting on you.
Keep company with me and you'll learn to live freely and lightly."
Matthew 11:28-30, MSG

I have worked against my to do list all week and I have barely made a dent. No boxes checked, nothings crossed off. The expectations I have laid in front of myself are too high. I want to do it all, but I am worn down and burned out.

I find excuses are easier than showing up; easier than making time.

The enemies scheming to keep me away from my Bible worked. I have looked at it as another need on my to do list, rather than true rest. I have spent my time, hours upon hours pouring over TV and social media in search of a way to quiet my mind and heart. Yet, I find myself back in the very place I started; overwhelmed by the noise of the world.

My heart becomes undone without His Word.

In fact He sent Jesus to give us freedom from legalistic rules. There is no requirement to open our Bibles every day because a box on our to do list can't save us. However, He <u>wants</u> you to long to open its pages and inhale His Truth, so much so, that He places a desire within us. God knows that the very words you hold in your hand will radically change your life.

If we cannot find true rest when we open, hear, or speak His Word then we will never know true rest and always wrestle to find it somewhere else. From experience I can tell you there is no better place to quiet your mind than in the pages of Scripture.

For us, His children, Bible study should never equal burden; it should <u>equal joy</u>.

Personally, I never wrestled with this until I had my third child. Owen was special, he loved to party all night and sleep all day. I was never more tired than I was in that season. Yet, it was in that place I found a new love for God's Word. That season changed everything. I could open my Bible and, even for just a few moments find lasting peace and rest.

Sure, the crying would continue and the sleepless nights lasted well past his first birthday, but finding mental and spiritual rest allowed me to find the physical rest I needed. I couldn't view my time in the Word as a chore, I had to ask God to change my heart, and see His Word as beautiful rest for this weary mom.

Even now as my children are older and the sleepless nights are behind me, I know when my shoulders are tight and my mind is worn down from the world around me. There is true and lasting rest to be found in Christ. True and lasting peace found when I open the pages of Scripture and let God breathe on me.

Books of the Bible

Literary Genres of the Books of the Bible

Law/Pentateuch
Genesis
Exodus
Leviticus
Numbers
Deuteronomy

History
Joshua
Judges
Ruth
1 & 2 Samuel
1 & 2 Kings
1 & 2 Chronicles
Ezra
Nehemiah
Esther

Wisdom & Poetry
Job
Psalm
Proverbs
Ecclesiastes
Song of Solomon

Major Prophets
Isaiah
Jeremiah
Lamentations
Ezekiel
Daniel

Minor Prophets
Hosea
Joel
Amos
Obadiah
Jonah
Micah
Nahum
Habakkuk
Zephaniah
Haggai
Zechariah
Malachi

Gospels
Matthew
Mark
Luke
John

Church History
Acts

Pauline Epistles
Romans
1 & 2 Corinthians
Galatians
Ephesians
Philippians
Colossians
1 & 2 Thessalonians
1 & 2 Timothy
Titus
Philemon

General Epistles
Hebrews
James
1 & 2 Peter
1, 2 & 3 John
Jude

Apocalyptic
Revelation

Basic Bible Facts:

* 39 Old Testament Books and 27 New Testament Books
*Written by more than 40 authors, but inspired by one God.
*Written across 3 Continents.
*Written over a span of 1,500 years.
*Originally written in 3 different languges (Hebrew, Aramaic, Greek)

Notes

Part Two:

How to Study Your Bible

Bible Study tip #2

Print out a double-spaced copy of the passage or chapter you are studying, giving yourself 2-3 inch margins. This gives you room to write, mark and make all the notes that you need.

More Than Words

One of the greatest mistakes I made in my approach to Bible study was believing that it was just another book on my bookshelf. The pages of Scripture are more than Words; they are life, instruction, warning, and promises all rolled into one.

In this section of the book we dive deeper into different Bible study methods and how to use them. The beauty of multiple methods is that we are able to focus on more than just the words and dig into context and application.

Any time we approach Scripture, our focus should be on facts before application. A phrase I have women repeat in my Bible studies is, "The Bible is not about me." Scripture isn't a grab bag that we can draw out what we want, what makes us feel good, or what fits how we like to live. We cannot approach our Bibles in such a way or we will be missing the power it holds.

Before I begin explaining each of these different methods please know I DO NOT use them all myself, and I don't expect you to either. What is important is that you find what works best for you. Also, I personally believe using just one style will not do the trick.

The first few methods are what we will call "surface scratchers":
- Verse Mapping
- Color Coding
- Soap Method
- Word Study
- Character Study

Then there are other methods which we will call "diggers":
- Inductive Method
- Homiletics
- Topical Study

(This is by no means an exhaustive list, just what we will cover.)

Each of these methods is useful when studying the Bible, but alone may leave gaps. When we study the Bible we should look at the whole picture and the best way in my opinion to do that is to study one book of the Bible at a time.

This gives us a greater understanding of each book as a whole and how it fits into the greater narrative that God is writing.

Let's begin to do the hard work, to dig deep in Scripture and ask God to teach us.

Which methods have you used to study before?

_____

_____

_____

What do you find daunting about the list of methods? Do you feel apprehension about using a more challenging method of study?

_____

_____

_____

Lay all of your fears out in prayer before the Lord, and ask for His help as you dig deeper into Scripture.

_____

_____

_____

_____

_____

Verse Mapping

When to use this method
If you are focusing on a key verse from your passage, this is a great time to use verse mapping. Also, if you are studying book by book, one chapter at a time; this method allows you to break it down verse by verse.

Why use this method
Verse Mapping helps you understand the verse in a deeper way, addressing the subject, predicate, verbs, repeated phrases, etc.

How to use this method
We ask key questions when we verse map:
Who is the verse talking about (tip: you and I, doesn't mean you or I)
What words that you need to look up the definition for?
What phrases are repeated?
Are there any action words?
What are some notes from other translations?

WHO? God

JOSHUA 1:9

WHO? Israelites (Joshua)

⁹ Have I not commanded you? Be strong and courageous. Do not be frightened, and do not be dismayed, for the LORD your God is with you wherever you go."

intimidated

Terrified tremble afraid

Repeated phrase

Where? everywhere

S.O.A.P. Method

When to use this method
This method is commonly used for daily Bible study.

Why use this method
It is broken down in a very simple format and is very appealing if you are just getting started with Bible study.

How to use this method

S - Scripture - Write out the Scripture you are studying, whether one verse or a passage.

O - Observations - What do you observe in the passage (this is the place to dig as deep as you can).

A - Application - What does this passage teach you about God? How does it apply to your life?

P - Prayer - Turn the verse or passage into a prayer.

For Practice:

S - Scripture

_____
_____

O - Observations

_____
_____
_____

A - Application

_____
_____

P - Prayer

_____
_____

Color Coding

When to use this method

Coloring coding is a great method to use daily with your Bible study. This process allows you to really slow down and think about what you are reading. There are many different color charts available; one is included for you.

When you print out a copy of the Scripture you are studying. Even in your Bible, use the color chart to analyze the passage.

Why use this method

Using the color coding system enhances words and allows you to gain a greater understanding of what you are studying. Use this method in conjunction with other methods.

How to use this method

Use highlighters, crayons, or colored pencils for this method. (You can check out the recommended tools guide in the back of this book for my favorites.)

1. Print a copy of your passage or chapter; or use your Bible.
2. Fill in your color chart using your highlighters or colored pencils.
3. Begin slowly reading the passage, looking for the different prompts to color or mark. (i.e., historical context, locations, God's Promises, Words Jesus spoke, prophecy, etc.)
4. Soak in the verses slowly so you don't miss any pockets of truth.
5. Remember, there is no one perfect way to do color coding; tweak until you have a a system that works well for you. Your color coded passage will likely look different from someone else's.

Bible Study ♥ Color Chart

- ○ Sin/Disobedience
- ○ Warning
- ○ Instruction
- ○ Worship/Faith, Righteous Action
- ○ Historical Events
- ○ People and Places
- ○ Promises of God/Character of God, Action of God
- ○ Jesus, Christ Image in the Old Testament
- ○ Prophecy
- ○ Prophecy fulfilled
- ○ Keywords
- ○ Wow Truths
- ○ This fuels how I should live

@displayinggrace ♥ displayinggrace.com

Word Study

When to use this method

This is a great method to use when you want to study a specific word. For example, Praise; this word may seem simple but there is much we can learn about them from Scripture.

Why use this method

Understanding the original meaning of a word is extraordinarily helpful when it comes to comprehending what you are studying.

How to use this method

Choose the word or words you would like to study. Use the format below as a template when completing a word study. You can find more information on Logos, FaithLife, biblehub.com, biblegateway.com.

Word :_____

English Definition: _____
_____

Hebrew or Greek Definition: _____
_____

How many times is the word used in Scripture? _____

How does this enhance your understanding of this verse or passage?
_____
_____
_____

Character Study

When to use this method

Character studies are a great tool when you want to dig deeper into the life of someone in the Bible. However, I have to stress this one fact; we aren't learning about their stories to know more about them, we are uncovering truths about them to know more about who God is.

Why use this method

A great time to use this method is when reading through a chapter or passage. Each character you encounter in your studies may not fit the bill of a character study because there is not enough information available, but others, however, are great to study, for example, Paul.

How to use this method

With a character study you want to find as much information as you can.

What verses is this person mentioned in?

Did they write a book of the Bible?

Did they have a personal encounter with God?

What are the historical facts about the person?

What does their story teach you about God?

Your Bible concordance, Bible handbook, or Bible encyclopedia may be needed for some of this information.

Remember: There is a great deal we can learn about the people of Scripture; they were flesh and blood just like you and me. Character studies can be very helpful for telling of who God is and how He loves us.

*Use our Character Study Sheet on pg. 39 to help you dig deeper.

Bible Character Study

Name of Character: _____

Scripture References	Biographical information: (i.e., birth place, culture, etc.)	Major Events	Observations about their personality/character	What do they teach us about the Gospel?

Inductive Study Method

When to use this method

The Inductive method is a great way to dig deeper into Scripture and is the one I recommend and I personally use most often.

Why use this method

This method gets to the heart of the passage context by observing the facts and treating the passage as more than mere words on a page.

How to use this method

This method will take more than one session to complete, you will work through this process over the course of days or weeks.

Five Steps of Inductive Bible Study:

1. **5 W's - (Context)**
    - **Who**   Who wrote it and to whom was it written?
    - **What**   What style? Wisdom Literature, Historical, Prophecy, Gospel, Epistles, Apocalyptic, Church History
    - **When**   When was it written?
    - **Where**   Historical location where the events take place
    - **Why**   Why was it written?

2. Observation/Comprehension (Discover) - Reading for detail, what does the verse/passage literally say?

- Printed Copy of Scripture (double spaced, 12 point font) This gives you this room to write thoughts and make marks you need.
- Repetitive reading - Read it multiple times over a period of time this allows you to become familiar with the text.
- Make notes of:
    1. Repeated Words or Phrases

2. Attributes of God
3. Lists
4. Words you don't understand
5. Transition words (Therefore, if/then, likewise, but, because, or in the same way)
6. Verbs and conjunctions

- English Dictionary - look up the definition of words you are reading.
- Other Translations - Literal translations such as NASB & ESV (most word for word), KJV, CSB, or NKJV.

3. Interpretation (Uncover)- What does it mean? (attempt to interpret the verse/passage on your own before consulting commentaries, study notes, Bible studies or paraphrases)

- Cross-Reference Verses - These verses are located in the margins or at the bottom of the page in your Bible.
- Paraphrasing - This is your interpretation; it helps you take what you have uncovered for yourself and focus on what is being said in the passage. Once you have created your interpretation then you can compare it to someone else's. It is vital that you wrestle with the text first.
- Historical, study notes, commentaries, paraphrase.

4. Application (Implement)-

1. What does this passage teach me about God?
2. How does this aspect of God's character change my view of who I am?
3. What should my response be?

Topical Study Method

When to use this method

Use this method for a specific topic you would like to study in Scripture (i.e. the Law, the Resurrection, persecution, etc.)

Why use this method

This is a great method to dig deep into a specific topic. You will need a wider variety of resources for this type of study such as, Bible dictionary, Bible atlas, Logos software, or a concordance.

How to use this method

1. Search Scripture for the verses pertaining to this topic. (biblegateway.com is a great resource for this.) Be careful not to leave anything out.
2. Once you have your list of verses you can then use verse mapping and other Scripture versions to help you understand the verses. Looking up cross reference verses may help as well.
3. Make a list of the facts you encounter about the topic you have chosen and the verses where you learned them.

Topic Suggestions:

Money

Prayer

Community

Worship

Marriage

Divorce

Obedience

Homiletics Study Method

When to use this method?

This study method is great to use if you are interested in getting to the facts of Scripture, as well as if you are studying to teach Scripture.

Why use this method?

This method will help you gain a deeper understanding of the passage of Scripture, focusing on the details before application points.

How to use this method?

Homiletics focuses on the facts of the passage.
The process is broken into five categories:

- **Content:** JUST THE FACTS (the who, what, when, where, NOT why). In the passage or chapter you will write down 10-20 pieces of content.

- **Divisions:** A summary of the details; divide your 10-20 pieces of content into 2-4 divisions or categories (write supporting verses next to each division sentence). Sometimes your Bible can help you see the divisions of thought.

- **Subject Sentence:** Combine your divisions into one complete sentence that will summarize the entire passage. Ten words or less is best. This sentence should not spiritualize the passage, but simply be a summary of its facts. We are answering the question: *"What is the passage about?"*

- **Aim:** The aim is your main teaching point and should be short, clearly taught in the passage and, most importantly, doctrinally correct. Use only the facts to get the aim.

- **Application:** Application is getting to the heart of the reader. How can we practically apply this truth to our lives and to the lives of those we are teaching? You should have one application for each division.

Are you confused yet? Let's work through it together.

Homiletics Example Passage: 1 John 1

Content: (Who, What, When, Where, the Facts of the Passage)

1. Word of life, from the beginning. (vs. 1)
2. They have seen and touched the word of life. (vs.1)
3. They testify to the Word made manifest. (vs. 2)
4. Proclaim eternal life. (vs. 2)
5. They share the Gospel in order for others to have fellowship with Jesus Christ. (v. 3)
6. Writing to them that their joy may be complete (v. 4)
7. God is light, there is no darkness in Him at all. (v. 5)
8. We lie if we say we have fellowship with God yet walk in darkness. (v.6)
9. If we walk in light the blood of Jesus cleanses us from sin. (v.7)
10. If we walk in light we have fellowship with one another. (v.7)
11. If we say we have no sin, the truth is not in us. (v. 8)
12. If we confess our sins, He is faithful and just to forgive. (v.9)
13. If we say we have never sinned, we make Him a liar. (v.10)

Divisions:

1. The Word of Life, Jesus, who was in the beginning, was made manifest to bring eternal life; and His life was witnessed by the disciples.
2. God is light, when we walk in light there can be no darkness in us. Our sin will keep us in darkness without the forgiveness through Christ's redeeming work on the cross.

Subject Sentence:

Jesus' shed blood reveals the darkness of sin and allows man to walk in light.

Aim:

If we confess our sins, the blood of Christ cleanses us. His forgiveness allows us to walk in light, as God is in the light.

Application:

1. We can trust the Gospel message because the disciples witnessed first hand the Word made flesh.
2. God's light reveals the darkness of sin within us but through the redemptive power of Christ we can walk in the light with God.

Once you have worked through the process of Homiletics you can more effectively teach and develop study questions. What I love about this method is how it keeps you focused on the facts because context is vital in Scripture. We cannot overlook the facts and move straight to application. Focusing on the facts helps us rightly divide the Word (2 Timothy 2:15).

**It is worth noting that this process will take time and is meant to stretch you and allow God to teach you straight from His Word. Don't be afraid of this method and process; it is one that will richly bless you if you give it the chance.

Part Three:
Live it Out

Practical Quiet Times

One of the questions I get most often when I teach is, "How to do I find time to read my Bible, study and have quiet time every day?" Simultaneously, the number one statement I hear is, "I just don't have time."

I get it. I see you. I have been there too. But, here is the truth - we *do* have time. The struggle is to find and claim it for reading God's Word.

We have placed extraordinary expectations on ourselves as women to be super heroes. We want to do it all, and do it all just like Wonder Woman. The thing is, we are not her, plus she is fictional, so there. The beauty is God is not asking or expecting that from us. He does, however, want our time for His purpose and glory.

For me personally it became a question of what was more important to me, sleeping late each day or getting up and making my mornings about being in the Word. I have had seasons where it became a question of what is more important during nap time? For some of you it may be what is more important as I close out my day. Regardless, you have to ask yourself the same question.

My quiet time is in the morning before the chaos of the day begins and it is still and quiet.

Each of our times in the Word will look different and there is no right or wrong time, no right or wrong place to be in the Word. The important part is that you find yourself there.

The car pool line.
Listening to an audio reading on the way to work.
Your lunch break.
After the kids are fast asleep.

All of the methods I have shown you in this book may not be used every day. Some days you may simply read while on others you may study inductively. You will find as you start to spend time reading your Bible you will want more. God will stir the desire for His truth in you and draw you closer to Him.

What does quiet time practically look like?

*Always begin in prayer asking God to teach you and open your eyes to His truth.

*Read your passage or chapter for the day. If you have time make a few notes or use one of the Bible study methods.

*End in prayer thanking God for what He has taught you and for the time you were given to be in His Word.

Our quiet time doesn't have to be complicated and it certainly isn't something that we are merely checking off a list. Our time in God's Word has purpose. Just as we spend time with those we love to know them better, the same holds true for being in our Bibles daily.

Our phones need to be charged or they will not do what we need them to do. If we are not charged by the Word of God then we will be unable to do what God requires of us.

If we want to be the women God desires for us to be, then we must make time to be in His Word.

Bridging the Gap

It's time to lay down whatever it is you have been holding onto that comes between you and God's Word. Bridge the gap by laying down everything that you feel stands in your way: time, priorities, insecurities, unworthy thoughts, you name it. I spent too long believing I wasn't good enough to open God's Word and learn. It wasn't until I surrendered that insecurity that I found freedom every time I opened its pages.

Write your prayer below, date it and come back to it for a reminder every time you feel it creeping in again.

_____
_____
_____
_____
_____
_____
_____
_____
_____
_____
_____
_____
_____
_____
_____
_____

Bible Study tip #3

Ask these questions when applying Scripture to your life:
What does this teach me about God?
And, because this teaches me _____ about God,
how does it change me?

Defense Against Distraction

The greatest enemy of Bible study is distractions. I find that when I try to be focused I get quickly caught up with my to do list, a random thought that jumps, or the places I need to be during the day. Even, dare I say, the pitter pat of feet across the floor can distract us from being in His Word.

Distractions will come in all shapes and sizes. What you do with them is what matters most.

I have heard it said, "The greatest defense is a good offense." What will our offense be to distraction?

Offensive strategy to tame distractions:

-Turn your phone off and keep it in another room out of arm's reach.

-Keep a piece of paper next to you and when a thought pops up, quickly write it down but keep going.

-Put your to do list in its place. Remind yourself, "Those things can wait."

-Choose your study time in accordance to when your children are resting (early morning, nap time, or bedtime). You can also keep them busy with books of their own, or other busy projects like blocks, crafts, etc.

-Study in a low traffic area if you are easily distracted. Now that my children are a little older I can tuck myself upstairs away from the noise of the day.

The main thing we need to remember about distractions is that they are all subject to change. We get to decide how much we will allow them to pull us away from being in the Word.

Trust me, I understand distractions and have certainly competed with my fair share. I still struggle on a daily basis not to let things interfere with the most precious time of day I have.

Not all distractions are bad ones. Certainly we have to remember that the needs of our people are important, and God will honor the time given. I have spent many mornings in the chair holding my youngest with my Bible in hand. Even now if he wakes early he curls up in my lap in the stillness and rests while I read. Those moments are ones I cherish. I also know I can start again tomorrow or finish later in the afternoon or possibly before bed.

The goal is to make the time to be in the Word and trust that God will work out every detail.

What are a few ways you deal with your distractions? Or, what are some new ideas you can put into practice?

_____
_____
_____
_____
_____
_____
_____
_____
_____
_____
_____
_____
_____

Notes

"May the word of God dwell in you richly, teaching and admonishing one another in all wisdom, singing psalms and hymns and spiritual songs, with thankfulness in your hearts to God."

Colossians 3:16

Recommended Resources

Below are resources that I personally recommend and use. These are, however, not necessary to study your Bible.

Bibles
ESV Study Bible
LOGOs Bible Software
Life Application Study Bible
Parallel Bible (multiple versions in one)

Marking Tools
Sticky notes
Zebra Midliner Creative Markers
Sharpie Clear View Highlighter
Colored Pencils or Pens

Books for Your Library
Women of the Word By: Jen Wilkin
Warren Weirsbe Exposition Commentary
Christ - Centered Exposition
Bible Handbook
Illustrated Bible Dictionary

(Many or all can be found at your local library or church library)
You can also purchase them on amazon.com or christianbook.com

Fresh Start Bible Reading Plan

Day 1: James 1

Day 2: James 2

Day 3: James 3

Day 4: James 4

Day 5: James 5

Day 6: 1 Peter 1

Day 7: 1 Peter 2

Day 8: 1 Peter 3

Day 9: 1 Peter 4

Day 10: 1 Peter 5

Day 11: 2 Peter 1

Day 12: 2 Peter 2

Day 13: 2 Peter 3

Day 14: 1 John 1

Day 15: 1 John 2

Day 16: 1 John 3

Day 17: 1 John 4

Day 18: 1 John 5

Day 19: 2 John 1

Day 20: 3 John 1

Day 21: 1 Tim. 1

Day 22: 1 Tim. 2

Day 23: 1 Tim. 3

Day 24: 1 Tim. 4

Day 25: 1 Tim. 5

Day 26: 1 Tim. 6

Day 27: 2 Tim. 1

Day 28: 2 Tim. 2

Day 29: 2 Tim. 3

Day 30: 2 Tim. 4

For more Bible Reading Plans including our yearly plans check out
www.displayinggrace.com/free-resources

Notes

Notes

Displaying Grace

Equipping women to thrive in their walk with Jesus.

Follow along with us with the NEW Bible reading plan. Grab yours FREE at www.displayinggrace.com

Plus, be sure to check out our other resources in the shop, as well as follow along with us on social media @displayinggrace

Want to learn more?
Check out our Youtube Channel for free videos or grab our Consumed Life course on teachable beginning in January 2019!

www.ingramcontent.com/pod-product-compliance
Lightning Source LLC
Chambersburg PA
CBHW080449110426
42743CB00016B/3332